Hello Kitty®
Felt
Activity Book

by Deborah Schecter

Scholastic Inc.

New York Toronto London Auckland Sydney
Mexico City New Delhi Hong Kong Buenos Aires

Illustrations: Yancey C. Labat

Felt projects created by Deborah Schecter

ISBN 0-439-32842-X

12 11 10 9 8 7 6 5 4 3 2 1   2 3 4 5 6/0

Printed in the U.S.A.
First Scholastic printing, April 2002

Table of Contents

Get Ready for Felt Fun with Hello Kitty!

Hello Kitty and her pal Tracy are ready to share lots of fantastic projects with you using soft, fuzzy felt! What would you like to do first? Join them on an overnight camp-out or on a super-cool ride at an amusement park? Or how about taking a trip around the world with Hello Kitty and Tracy? You can visit a castle in England, dress up in a grass skirt in hot, sunny Hawaii, or stop over in Paris to pick up the latest fab fashions!

So get set for nonstop felt fun with Hello Kitty and Tracy!

Let's Get Started

On the pages that follow, you'll find all sorts of fun and easy projects you can make with the soft, fuzzy felt and three stencils in your pack—a Hello Kitty Stencil, a Tracy Stencil, and a Super Stars and Flowers Stencil. If you run out of felt, you can always stop by your local craft or hobby store and pick up some more.

Having Fun with Your Felt Projects:

Since most of the felt projects you make in this book are flat, you'll want to use a flat surface to play with them. You can set up a scene on your desktop for Hello Kitty and Tracy to play on, or use your carpeted floor. There are also some fun, three-dimensional projects, such as finger puppets and a merry-go-round. These projects come to life with your hands-on help!

P.S. Save those scraps! Don't throw away bits and pieces of leftover felt. You can always use them when you make new projects!

The following stuff will come in handy for making the felt projects in this book:
- Scissors
- Fabric craft glue
- Stapler
- Tape
- Cardboard
- Toothpicks
- Cotton ball
- Ruler

To decorate your felt projects, here are some things to have handy:
- Markers
- Fabric paint
- Glitter
- Itty-bitty buttons
- Sequins
- Craft feathers

Make Hello Kitty and Tracy with Your Stencil Patterns:

Before making all the fun projects in this book, start by creating Hello Kitty and her pal Tracy.

What You Do:

1. Place your Hello Kitty or Tracy stencil on top of a piece of felt. Use your white felt for Hello Kitty (we've used pink felt in this book so that Hello Kitty stands out better) and your black felt for Tracy.

Hello Kitty Stencil

Tracy Stencil

2. Hold the stencil firmly in place with one hand. With your other hand, trace inside the stencil with a pencil. If you're using black felt, trace with a yellow fine-tip marker instead.

(continued on next page)

3. Lift off the stencil. Then cut out the shape along the outline you just traced.

4. On your Hello Kitty cutout, draw her face using markers or fabric paint, or use itty-bitty pieces of felt.

5. For Tracy's face, trace this pattern onto paper and cut it out. Then trace it onto white felt and cut it out.

What You Need:
- Stencils
- Felt
- Pencil, or yellow fine-tip marker
- Scissors
- Markers or fabric paint (optional)
- Paper
- Fabric craft glue
- Buttons, sequins, glitter, craft feathers, or other decorative materials (optional)

To Dress Up Hello Kitty and Tracy

1. Hello Kitty loves clothes! With your stencils and felt, you can make oodles of outfits and pretty bows to dress her up in style! Look through the pages of this book for some fabulous fashion ideas. For Tracy, use the overalls pattern on your Hello Kitty Stencil and decorate it for him.

2. Use craft glue to attach decorations cut from scraps of felt, itty-bitty buttons, sequins, glitter, craft feathers, and other fun stuff!

5

Hello Kitty says:

It's easy to mix and match outfits! Just press a felt outfit onto my felt cutout and it will stay in place. When it's time to change my outfits, just lift one off and replace with another one!

Hello Kitty and Tracy Finger Puppets:

Hello Kitty and Tracy are ready for action! Why not make them into finger puppets and help them come to life?

What You Do:

1. Use your Hello Kitty Stencil to trace and cut out two identical Hello Kitty shapes from your felt. Trace two more identical patterns using your Tracy Stencil and cut them out.

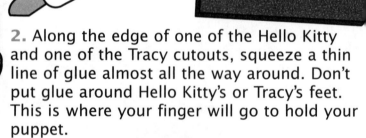

2. Along the edge of one of the Hello Kitty and one of the Tracy cutouts, squeeze a thin line of glue almost all the way around. Don't put glue around Hello Kitty's or Tracy's feet. This is where your finger will go to hold your puppet.

What You Need:

- Stencils
- Felt
- Pencil
- Scissors
- Fabric craft glue
- Decorative materials (fabric paint or glitter)

3. Place the matching cutouts on top of the glue and press them together. Let them dry.

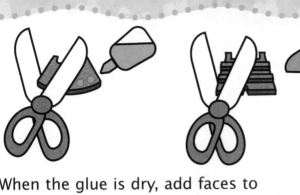

4. When the glue is dry, add faces to your Hello Kitty and Tracy puppets, just as you did on page 4. Then, use your stencils to make outfits for the two friends, just as you did on page 5. You can decorate them using felt scraps and other materials.

Hello Kitty says:
Now slip Tracy or me on your fingers, and let us do the talking!

Hello Kitty's
Creative Corner

Hello Kitty Paints a Picture:

Hello Kitty loves to express herself in lots of ways. Today, she's painting a picture of her pal Tracy!

What You Do:

1. Start with your felt cutout of Hello Kitty from your Hello Kitty Stencil (see pages 3–4).

2. Now make a felt artist's smock for Hello Kitty to wear using the smock pattern from your Hello Kitty Stencil.

What You Need:
- Stencils
- Felt
- Pencil
- Scissors
- Fabric paint or markers
- Hole punch
- Fabric craft glue
- Cardboard
- Ruler

8

3. Hello Kitty wears her smock when she paints, so it has splotches of paint on it! If you like, make paint splotches on your Hello Kitty smock by using fabric paint or markers.

4. To make Hello Kitty's paint palette, cut out a felt shape like the one pictured here.

Paint Palette

5. To make pans of paint for Hello Kitty's palette, use a hole punch to make felt dots in different colors, or cut color dots out with scissors. Glue them to Hello Kitty's paint palette.

6. Make Hello Kitty a paintbrush by cutting one out from your felt like the one shown. Cut itty-bitty slits in the brush part to make bristles. Dab on "paint" using markers or fabric paint.

Paintbrush

Here's More:

You can make an easel for Hello Kitty, the painter.

What You Do:

1. On a piece of cardboard, draw a shape like the one you see here. It looks like the letter "A" with an extra leg. A ruler will help you make straight lines.

←slits→

2. Poke the tip of your scissors into the middle of the shape to cut out the inside. Then cut two slits, as shown.

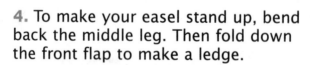

3. Color your easel with markers or paint.

4. To make your easel stand up, bend back the middle leg. Then fold down the front flap to make a ledge.

5. Cut a square of white felt for Hello Kitty to paint her picture on. You can make any picture you want using your felt, paint, or markers. Hello Kitty has made a picture of Tracy.

Hello Kitty Makes Music:

Strike up the band and dance to Hello Kitty and Tracy's beat.

To Make a Xylophone

1. Hello Kitty likes to play the xylophone! To make one for her, cut out a shape like this from your felt.

Xylophone

2. Now cut little rectangles in different colors to fit on the shape. Glue them on. These are your musical notes.

3. Make musical hammers like the ones shown for Hello Kitty to play on her xylophone. Use a hole punch to make two felt dots for the tips of the hammers, or use round sequins. Glue them to two small strips of felt.

To Make a Drum

1. Can you guess what Tracy likes to play? The drum! To make one, cut out a square from your felt.

2. Now decorate the drum using scraps of felt. Don't forget to cut little black sticks for Tracy's drumsticks!

What You Need:

- **Felt**
- **Pencil**
- **Scissors**
- **Fabric craft glue**
- **Hole punch, or round sequins**

11

Hello Kitty Puts on a Play:

It's opening night and Hello Kitty is the star of her school play!

What You Do:

1. Start with your felt cutout of Hello Kitty from your stencil (see pages 3–4).

2. What will Hello Kitty be in the play? A queen! Will you help make her costume? Use your Hello Kitty Stencil to trace and cut out a felt gown.

What You Need:

- **Stencils**
- **Felt**
- **Pencil**
- **Scissors**
- **Decorative materials (markers, fabric paint, glitter, sequins, tiny beads, foil)**
- **Fabric craft glue**
- **Shoe box lid**

Crown

3. To make Hello Kitty a royal crown, cut out a shape like this from your felt.

4. The queen needs a royal scepter. You'll find one on your Tracy Stencil.

5. Decorate Hello Kitty's gown, crown, and scepter with felt scraps, glitter, sequins, itty-bitty beads, pieces of foil, or other decorations. Make Hello Kitty a costume fit for a queen!

6. Where will Hello Kitty put on her play? She needs a stage! Glue white felt to the inside of a shoe box lid. Then glue felt curtains of a different color to the top and each end of the lid.

If Hello Kitty is the Queen, who will Tracy be? Decide, then make a costume for Tracy, too.

13

Hello Kitty says:

It's show time—are you ready for my entrance?

Hello Kitty Goes to Dance Class:

Hello Kitty is always busy! Today she is a ballerina!

What You Do:

1. Trace two identical patterns of Hello Kitty and cut them out. Along the edge of one of the cutouts, squeeze a thin line of glue *almost* all the way around. Don't put glue around Hello Kitty's feet. Stick the other cutout on top of the first one and let them dry.

2. Use your Hello Kitty Stencil to trace and cut out a tutu for Hello Kitty to wear.

What You Need:

- Stencils
- Felt
- Pencil
- Scissors
- Fabric craft glue
- Decorative materials (markers, fabric paint, glitter, sequins)
- Hole punch
- Pipe cleaner
- Spool of thread

3. Decorate Hello Kitty's tutu using glitter or fabric paint.

14

4. To make a pretty head-band, cut a small strip of felt to fit on Hello Kitty's head. Use a hole punch to make little felt dots and glue them to the strip. Make colorful felt streamers to glue to Hello Kitty's headband, too.

5. Glue one end of a pipe cleaner inside the bottom of your Hello Kitty cutout. Let the glue dry.

6. Poke the other end of the pipe cleaner through the hole in a spool of thread.

7. Bend the pipe cleaner twice to make a handle, as shown.

8. To make Hello Kitty spin and twirl, turn the handle as you hold the spool!

15

Hello Kitty says:
A one, a two, a three, let's dance!

Hello Kitty in the Great Outdoors

Hello Kitty Goes Apple Picking:

It's a crisp, fall day—perfect for apple picking in the country!

To Make Hello Kitty Apple-decorated Overalls

1. Start with your felt cutout of Hello Kitty from your stencil (see pages 3–4).

2. Hello Kitty wears overalls when she goes apple picking. Use your Hello Kitty Stencil to trace the overalls pattern onto felt and cut it out.

What You Need:
- **Stencils**
- **Felt**
- **Pencil**
- **Scissors**
- **Red construction paper**
- **Fabric craft glue**

3. To decorate Hello Kitty's overalls, make a little red apple by cutting a small circle out of red construction paper. Then cut a little leaf out of your green felt. Glue the leaf onto the red apple, and then glue the apple to Hello Kitty's overalls.

16

To Make an Apple Tree

1. To make an apple tree, cut out a black felt tree trunk with some branches. Cut out a puffy green felt shape like this for the top of the tree, and glue it onto the trunk.

2. Now fill the tree with ripe, red apples. Use the apple shape from your Tracy Stencil to trace and cut apples out of red construction paper. Add a green felt leaf to each apple. Glue the apples to the tree.

3. How will Hello Kitty and Tracy reach the apples? They need a ladder! Cut two long, thin strips of felt. Then cut a bunch of short strips. Arrange them like this and glue them together.

Hello Kitty Goes on a Picnic:

After apple picking, it's time for lunch! Would you help Hello Kitty and Tracy pack their picnic?

To Make a Picnic Blanket

1. Cut a piece of felt in half. Then, fold one of the pieces in half the short way.

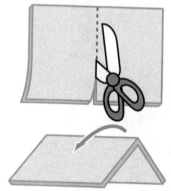

2. Starting at the fold, cut five slits, equally spaced, into the felt. Cut each slit until you're about 1" from the open ends. Then reopen the felt.

3. Now cut six strips of felt in different colors, each about 4½" long and ½" wide.

What You Need:
- Felt
- Scissors
- Ruler
- Fabric craft glue
- Stencils
- Pencil
- Glitter

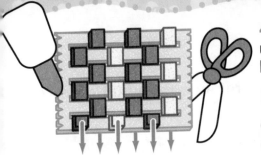

4. Weave each strip of felt over and under each of the slits you cut in the big piece of felt.

5. Glue down the ends of each strip.

6. To put a fringe on your blanket, cut lots of slits, side by side, into each end.

To Pack a Picnic Lunch

1. Hello Kitty and Tracy pack sandwiches to munch on for lunch. First, cut little squares of white felt for bread. Cut little pink squares to make the sandwich meat. Add some green felt for lettuce, if you like. Then glue your sandwich fixin's together.

2. What's for dessert? Apple pie, of course! Use your circle pattern from your Tracy Stencil to cut a white felt circle for the pie. Make little pink half circles for apple slices. Add the apple slices to your pie. Then crisscross the pie with white felt strips of crust and sprinkle them with some "cinnamon" glitter.

19

Hello Kitty says:

Spread everything out on the picnic table. Lunch is ready. Let's eat!

Hello Kitty Goes Camping:

Hello Kitty and Tracy are going on an overnight camp-out. How exciting!

To Make a Sleeping Bag

1. Start with your felt cutout of Hello Kitty from your stencil (see pages 3–4). Place your Hello Kitty cutout on a piece of felt of another color. Cut a felt strip that's a little wider and longer than Hello Kitty is.

2. Dab some glue along the outer edges of the felt strip.

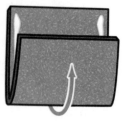

3. Fold up one end of the strip, as shown. Then fold down the other end to make a pillow. Let the glue dry.

What You Need:

- Stencils
- Felt
- Pencil
- Scissors
- Fabric craft glue
- Orange construction paper or tissue paper
- Toothpicks

To Make a Campfire

1. Cut a bunch of strips out of your black felt to make sticks. Crisscross them in different ways and glue them together.

2. Cut out a flame shape from orange paper for your campfire and glue it to the stick pile.

Hello Kitty says:

Let's make toasted marshmallows for a camp-out treat! First, cut out little squares of white felt. Then glue the squares to the ends of toothpicks, which will be your toasting sticks (or use tiny real sticks, if you like).

21

Hello Kitty Picks Flowers:

Hello Kitty surprises Tracy with a bunch of beautiful blooms that she picked herself.

To Design a Basic Flower Bud

1. Use different flower shapes from your Super Stars and Flowers Stencil to trace and cut out felt flowers.

Super Stars and Flowers Stencil

2. Cut out green leaves from your Tracy Stencil and add your own stems. They can be any shape or size you like.

3. Now design different kinds of flowers. You can glue smaller flower buds onto larger ones, mix and match colors, or do whatever you like! Glue the parts together.

4. Decorate your flowers using fabric paint, glitter, sequins, and more.

What You Need:
- Stencils
- Felt
- Pencil
- Scissors
- Fabric craft glue
- Decorative materials (fabric paint, glitter, sequins)
- Ruler
- Green toothpicks

22

To Design a 3-D Flower with Leaves

1. Cut a strip of felt about 2" long and 1" wide.

2. Make a fringe by cutting lots of slits into the felt. Be careful not to cut all the way through the material.

3. Put some glue on the uncut part of the strip. Then wrap it around one end of a toothpick, which will be your flower stem.

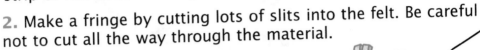

4. Add some green felt leaves.

5. If you like, make a center for your flower using felt scraps, glitter, sequins, or fabric paint.

To Make Friendly Garden Insects

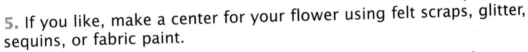

1. A butterfly and a dragonfly are fluttering over the flowers! Use your Super Stars and Flowers Stencil and felt to trace and cut out one or both of them.

2. Decorate your bugs with fabric paint, sequins, extra pieces of felt, or other decorative materials.

Hello Kitty's
Special Days

Hello Kitty's Class Trip:

Hello Kitty's class is going on a trip to the amusement park! First, everyone will ride on the merry-go-round!

What You Need:

- ● **Circular plastic lid or dish**
- ● **2 Pencils (one sharpened, one unsharpened)**
- ● **Scissors**
- ● **Felt**
- ● **Lightweight cardboard**
- ● **Fabric craft glue**
- ● **Decorative materials (markers, strips of felt, glitter, sequins)**
- ● **Stencils**

To Make a Merry-go-round

1. Using a circular plastic lid or dish, trace and cut out a circle from a piece of felt. Trace and cut out the same size circle from a piece of cardboard. Then glue the circles together.

2. Cut a small hole in the center of the circle of cardboard and felt. Make sure the hole is just big enough to fit the eraser end of a pencil.

3. Cut a bunch of thin felt strips in a few different colors. Glue them around the circle, to the cardboard side.

4. Now make Hello Kitty and Tracy cutouts (see pages 3–4) and clothes (see page 5) and glue them to the ends of the thin strips of felt. Let them dry.

Bottom view

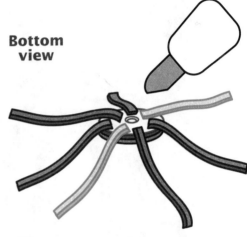

Top view

(continued on next page)

5. Add decorations to the top of the merry-go-round's circle of cardboard and felt, if you like. Then, poke the eraser end of your pencil through the hole.

6. To make your merry-go-round spin, hold the pencil between your hands, and slowly roll it back and forth. Wheeee!

Hello Kitty says:

Hop on the merry-go-round for a fun ride!

Hello Kitty Wins a Prize:

Hello Kitty plays a game at the amusement park and wins! What prize will she pick?

What You Do:

1. What kind of toy plush prize do you think Hello Kitty would like? A Teddy bear or a cutie bird? Take your pick! Then trace and cut out two of the same shapes from your Tracy Stencil on any color felt you like.

2. Along the edge of one of your shapes, squeeze a thin line of glue *almost*, but not quite, all the way around. Leave a small opening at the bottom.

3. Line up the two cutout shapes and press them together.

4. When the glue is dry, put a cotton ball inside your toy plush through the area that you didn't glue shut (a pencil will help you poke it in). Then glue the opening closed.

What You Need:

- **Stencils**
- **Felt**
- **Scissors**
- **Fabric craft glue**
- **Cotton ball**
- **Pencil**
- **Decorative materials (fabric paint, glitter, sequins)**

5. Decorate your toy plush with felt scraps, fabric paint, glitter, sequins, and more!

Sweet Treats and Bright Balloons:

What's next at the amusement park? Hello Kitty buys some sweet treats. And Tracy? A bunch of big, bright balloons!

To Make Cotton Candy

1. Pull off a piece from a large cotton ball—this will be your cotton candy.

2. What color cotton candy would you like? Pink? Blue? Maybe a swirly mix of colors? Use markers or fabric paint to dab color onto your cotton ball.

3. Cut a triangular shape out of felt to make a cone for your cotton candy. Dab on some color here, too, with markers or paint.

4. Glue the cotton candy to the cone.

What You Need:

- A large cotton ball
- Decorative materials (markers, fabric paint, glitter)
- Felt
- Scissors
- Fabric craft glue
- Stencils
- Toothpicks
- Yarn or string

To Make a Tasty Lollipop

1. What flavor lollipop would you like? Bubble-gum pink? Licorice black? Pick a color of felt and cut out a circle from your Tracy Stencil.

2. Use fabric paint, markers, or glitter to make swirls and other decorations on your lollipop.

3. Add a stick to your lollipop by gluing a toothpick to the back of the circle.

To Make Bright Balloons

1. Cut out colorful felt balloon shapes like the one pictured here.

2. Glue a piece of yarn or string to the back of each balloon.

3. Decorate the balloons, if you like.

29

Hello Kitty **says:**

The amusement park was so much fun!

Trick-or-treat with Hello Kitty:

For Halloween, Hello Kitty and Tracy are dressing up!

To Make Hello Kitty's Witch Costume

1. Hello Kitty is going trick-or-treating as a witch. She needs a tall, black witch's hat and a black dress to wear. Use your Hello Kitty Stencil to trace and cut out Hello Kitty's witch's dress and hat for her.

2. Decorate Hello Kitty's costume using felt scraps, glitter, and fabric paint. Use your stencil to make a felt bow for Hello Kitty's hat, too!

3. To be a witch, Hello Kitty needs a broom to ride on! Will you make her one using the broom shape from your Tracy Stencil? Attach pieces of straw raffia, or strips cut from a brown paper bag to the broom, if you like.

To Make Tracy's Clown Costume

1. Guess what Tracy is going trick-or-treating as? A clown! To make a silly clown hat for Tracy to wear, use the witch's hat from your Hello Kitty Stencil on a bright color of felt and cut it out.

2. What funny things will you glue on Tracy's hat? How about streamers, sequins, or a pom-pom!

3. Now make Tracy some funny overalls to wear using the overalls from your Hello Kitty Stencil. Don't forget to decorate them in a silly way!

To Make a Trick-or-treat Bag

Now Hello Kitty and Tracy need a bag to hold their Halloween candy! Use the pumpkin from your Super Stars and Flowers Stencil to make a trick-or-treat bag out of felt. Add a handle by cutting out a small strip of felt and gluing it to the back of the pumpkin cutout. Then, decorate your pumpkin's face.

What You Need:

- Stencils
- Felt
- Pencil, or a fine-tip yellow marker
- Scissors
- Decorative materials (fabric paint, glitter, straw raffia or a brown paper bag, pom-poms, sequins)
- Fabric craft glue

31

Hello Kitty says:

What will you dress up as for Halloween?

Around the World
with Hello Kitty

Hello Kitty Visits a Castle:

Hello Kitty and Tracy are taking a trip around the world! First stop—England. Hello Kitty and Tracy will visit a castle built long ago!

What You Do:

1. To make the three towers of your castle, cut three rectangles about 4½" long by 3" wide out of felt.

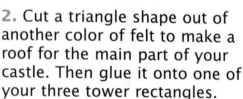

What You Need:

- Felt
- Ruler
- Scissors
- Fabric craft glue
- Decorative materials (fabric paint, markers, glitter)

2. Cut a triangle shape out of another color of felt to make a roof for the main part of your castle. Then glue it onto one of your three tower rectangles.

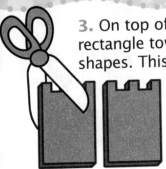

3. On top of each of the two remaining rectangle towers, cut out two small square shapes. This top portion is called a "turret."

4. Put one of these towers on each side of the main part of your castle.

5. Cut out windows for your castle from scraps of felt and glue them on.

6. Make a door from a piece of felt and glue it to the main part of your castle.

7. What else would you like to add to your castle? Maybe some flags? If so, cut them out from your felt and glue them onto your castle.

8. If you like, use markers, fabric paint, or glitter to decorate your castle.

Hello Kitty Visits Hawaii:

Aloha! Hello Kitty and Tracy are heading for sun and fun!

To Make Hello Kitty's Grass Skirt

1. Cut a small rectangle from your green felt.
2. Fringe the skirt by cutting short slits, side by side, into one side of the rectangle.

To Make Hello Kitty a Flower Necklace

Now make a *lei* (flower necklace) for Hello Kitty or Tracy to wear. Use your Super Stars and Flowers Stencil to cut out three small flowers from your felt. Place the flowers next to each other, overlapping them slightly and glue them together.

To Make a Pair of Sunglasses

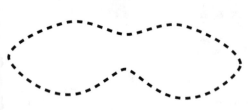

Hello Kitty needs a pair of cool shades! Trace the sunglasses pattern here onto a piece of paper and cut it out. Next, transfer the pattern onto your felt and cut it out. To make lenses, cut two small oval pieces out of dark felt and glue them to the sunglasses.

What You Need:

- Felt
- Scissors
- Stencils
- Fabric craft glue
- Paper
- Pencil

To Make a Palm Tree

Make a palm tree for Hello Kitty and Tracy to sit under. Cut a tree trunk out of dark felt. Then make big green felt leaves. Cut fringes in each leaf. Then glue the leaves to the tree.

Hello Kitty says:

Can you use your stencil to make me a fabulous bathing suit?

Hello Kitty Goes Shopping in Paris:

Ooh, la, la. Hello Kitty and Tracy are off to Paris to shop for the latest French fashions!

To Make Hello Kitty a Hat

1. First, Hello Kitty's off to the hat shop! There are so many pretty hats to choose from! Use your Hello Kitty Stencil to trace and cut out a hat shape from your felt.

2. Decorate the hat using felt flowers and bows, craft feathers, tiny buttons, sequins, glitter, fabric scraps, and other materials. Be as creative as you like!

What You Need:

- **Stencils**
- **Felt**
- **Pencil or fine-tip yellow marker**
- **Scissors**
- **Fabric craft glue**
- **Decorative materials (fabric paint, tiny buttons, sequins, doilies, craft feathers, glitter, fabric scraps)**

To Make Hello Kitty a Purse

In the next shop, the perfect purse catches Hello Kitty's eye. It's so pretty, she simply *must* buy it! Use your Hello Kitty Stencil to trace and cut out the purse shape from your felt. Glue the purse handle to the back of the bag, then decorate the purse using any materials you like.

To Make Hello Kitty Dresses and Bows

Hello Kitty is not done yet. She can't resist a fancy, frilly dress and, of course, some beautiful bows! Use your Hello Kitty Stencil to make these for her as well.

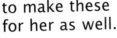

To Make Hello Kitty a Shopping Bag

Trace and cut out a shopping bag for Hello Kitty using your Tracy Stencil and some felt. Glue the handle onto the back of the bag and glue on a little button for decoration.

Hello Kitty **says:**

Oh! Hello Kitty, you look *trés jolie!* (That's French for "very pretty.")

Snack Time!

Now it's time for a snack at a *pâtisserie*. (That's French for "pastry shop.") Look at all the delicious desserts there are to choose from!

To Make *Petits Fours* (little cakes)

Cut a bunch of itty-bitty felt squares in different colors. Glue them together in layers. Put icing on your *petits fours* with markers or fabric paint.

To Make *Gâteaux* (cakes)

Cut out a square shape from your felt to make a layer cake and decorate it. Then cut out another shape like the one above to make a super-fancy cake and decorate it any way you like.

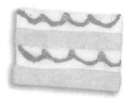

To Make *Bonbons* (candies)

Cut out little felt flowers, triangles, and circles. Layer them, then glue them together to create different kinds of candy. Decorate them, too!

Hello Kitty Travel Log:

Hello Kitty wants to remember her trip. Make her a journal to keep her memories in!

What You Do:

1. Cut out a felt rectangle. This will be the front and back cover of the journal.

2. Make pages by cutting paper into rectangles. Make sure they will fit inside your cover.

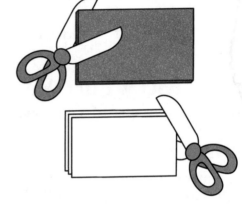

3. Fold the pages in half and nest them inside the cover. Staple along the left-hand side to bind the book. Decorate the front cover however you like.

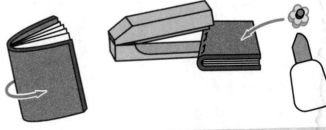

Extras You Need:
- Paper
- Stapler

Hello Kitty Accessories

If you love Hello Kitty accessories, no worries.
Now you can make some for yourself!

Hello Kitty Puff Pin:

Dress up any one of your own outfits with this nifty pin starring Hello Kitty!

What You Do:

1. Flatten out a cotton ball a little bit. Shape Hello Kitty's ears by pulling gently at each end of the cotton ball.

2. Poke the safety pin through one side of the cotton ball. If you're using a craft jewelry pin, glue the flat end to the cotton ball.

What You Need:

- **Cotton ball**
- **Safety pin or craft jewelry pin**
- **Fabric craft glue**
- **Felt scraps, markers, or fabric paint**
- **Stencils**

3. Decorate the other side of the ball with felt scraps, markers, or fabric paint to look like Hello Kitty. Don't forget to make Hello Kitty's bow!

Hello Kitty Bow-Barrette:

Make a bow to wear in your hair just like Hello Kitty's!

What You Do:

1. Trace the small flower pattern from your Super Stars and Flowers Stencil onto a piece of felt three times. Cut out each flower.

2. Trace the two leaves from your Tracy Stencil onto another piece of felt and cut them out.

3. Use your hole punch to punch out three circles for the flower centers and glue them to the top of each flower.

4. Glue the two leaves to the barrette, allowing them to overlap each end.

5. Arrange the three flowers you made in step 1 on the bow, overlapping the leaves and each other. When you like your design, glue the flowers to the barrette.

What You Need:
- **Stencils**
- **Felt**
- **Pencil**
- **Scissors**
- **Hole punch**
- **Fabric craft glue**
- **Barrette**

Hello Kitty says:

You can make other kinds of barrettes, too! Use your Super Stars and Flowers Stencil to make some more pretty designs.

Hello Kitty Pocket Purse:

With this pocket purse, you can take Hello Kitty with you wherever you go!

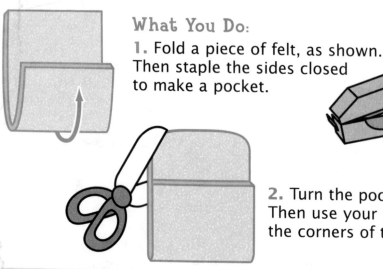

What You Do:

1. Fold a piece of felt, as shown. Then staple the sides closed to make a pocket.

2. Turn the pocket inside out. Then use your scissors to round the corners of the flap.

What You Need:

- **Felt**
- **Stapler**
- **Scissors**
- **Brass fastener or a small button**
- **Decorative materials (felt cutouts, fabric paint, markers, glitter, ribbon)**

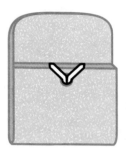

3. Use the point of your scissors to make a tiny hole in the front of the purse, as shown. Then, from the inside of the purse, poke the prongs of a brass fastener through the hole. If you don't have a brass fastener, ask a grown-up or an older friend to sew a little button onto your purse for you (you won't need to make a tiny hole).

4. Fold down the top flap. Then snip a little slit in the felt where the flap touches the brass fastener or button.

5. To close your purse, slip the prongs of the fastener through the slit and bend them down, or slip the button through the slit.

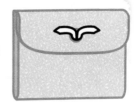

6. Decorate your purse with felt flowers, hearts, and stars, or whatever you like!

To wear your pocket
urse, thread it through your
lt. Or thread it through a
ece of ribbon that you can
around your waist.

43

Hello Kitty says:

You can take this little purse anywhere.

Toodles from Hello Kitty and Tracy

Hello Kitty and Tracy hope you've had as much fun as they've had making all the felt projects in this book. Which were your favorites? What other ideas can you dream up? Hello Kitty and Tracy are sure that you'll come up with lots of creative and crafty ideas!

Hugs and kisses!

Love,

xoxox Hello Kitty and Tracy